# Spooky Halloween Sticker Fun

# What am I?

Match each picture with its correct sticker.

See the candle glow.

Watch a sheet take shape.

Spy a toothy grin.

Catch one on the hop.

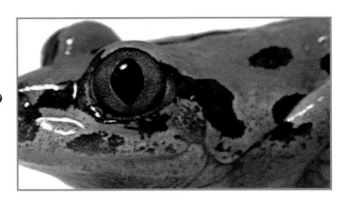

Spot a high flier.

Find a furry friend.

3

# Where are they?

Poltergeists are hiding things. Can you find …

… a third pumpkin, just like these?

… a second witch, riding her broom?

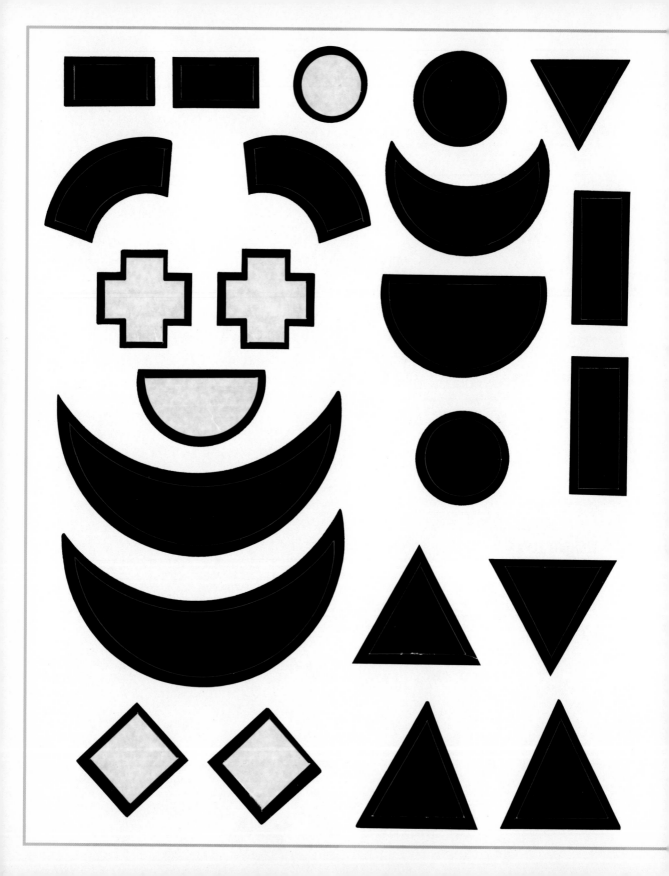

... four more candies, ready to eat?

... another ghost, all in white?

... three more stars, shining bright?

# Make up a face

Turn these fat pumpkins into jack-o'-lanterns.

One pumpkin begins to laugh,

and a second one joins the fun.

This pumpkin's had a surprise.

What about this one?

Or this?

Be creative! Look for spare stickers for these pumpkin faces.

# Lost and found

Wendy Witch is very forgetful. Can you help her find …

… her special book of spells?

… her magic broomstick?

… her clever cat?

… and her pointy hat?